HEALING THE BOND

Trauma with Your Mama

HEALING THE BOND

Trauma with Your Mama

by J. Chavae

This is for all of the women who are ready to heal, release, and transmute the pain into something beautiful.

Table of Contents

WHO AM I

I am J. Chavae.

My spirit has chosen to come to this earth in the body of a Black woman in order to help other women, particularly women who look like me and resonate with me, heal. I have been through many things in life that have allowed me the ability to speak
directly to the subject matters that I talk about.

I don't "think" that healing is powerful, beneficial, and
life-changing, I KNOW that it is because I have done it and I continue to do it every day.

I have survived many painful moments including but not limited to, familial trauma, rape, physical, mental, & verbal abuse,
depression, anxiety, and suicidal thoughts. Even through all of that, I am still here. I continue to come out of the other side with more healing knowledge every time.

WHY DO I DO THIS WORK

I do this work because this is a part of my soul purpose.
it honestly brings me great joy to share tools and insight with
people. It brings me even more joy when people's eyes light up when the
realizations of their lives hit them, when they see that joy is possible. When I
see people release through the outbreath or tears and can visibly see weight
lifted off of them, it validates
everything that I have been though, everything I have learned, and everything I do. I do the work because seeing people heal
themselves sparks an enormous amount of joy in my soul.

THE STORY BEHIND MOTHERS & DAUGHTERS COURSE

On January 2, 2018, I remember seeing a picture of my mother and saying to myself, "Wow, that woman looks pretty." I paused because honestly, I shocked myself. As I was looking at this woman in the picture, nothing in me associated her with "mother" or with a feeling of love or connectedness.

She didnt know me and I felt like I didnt know her. That realization honestly rubbed me the wrong way. My mother was alive and well and I did not have a relationship with her, let alone a proper one. I had been doing a great deal of self-work, including ancestral work, and here I was with a living mother that I didn't feel connected to....and it made me feel like shit.

Now, anyone who has known me since age 13 will know that I never really had a good relationship with my mother. I assumed the role of "mini mom" at a young age and interactions between my mother and I were often explosive and violent. I didn't really trust my mother with my emotions nor did I trust being vulnerable with her. For the longest time, I felt very defensive, irritated, or angry towards her. As I got older and stretched my wings of independence, our relationship got worse, including leaving her house for months, intense arguments, cursing each other out, not speaking for weeks at a time, or her attempting to make her trauma seem worse than mine aka invalidating my feelings, as she usually did.

Even when I moved back in with her in 2015, the same conversations kept getting repeated, which made me more upset (it really triggers me when people do not actually listen to me). I tried to "do better", but I felt like she was refusing to change. We ended up having many more arguments until another big explosion happened. I essentially told her my feelings on our relationship + more, and how I felt in a very brunt, harsh tone and language. The argument spilled over to text messages (mind you we were literally in the same house).

She essentially told me that she was giving me a deadline to get out of her house, even though she knew my financial status. I told her that if she kicked me out of her house that I would literally never speak to her again and that I would renounce my position as her daughter, as her first born... essentially, I would be dead to her.

We didnt speak for 3 days (again, I lived in her house). On the third day, she knocked on the bathroom door saying that she wanted to talk. I opened the door and she literally broke down crying. Through her tears she confessed to having abandonment issues, to not knowing how to communicate with me, to how she's felt that I have rejected her since I was 3 months old (I weaned myself off of her breast when I was 3 months old & I've always been a very independent child/person), and how she's tried her best from the time I was born. I just held her as she cried and let the words fall from her mouth.

In that moment, as I too cried holding my mother, I realized how much pain she has been through and how we had clearly not been seeing eye to eye all of these years. That was the first time I saw her humanness. I ended up moving out again and the relationship was kind of better after that, but still, I felt like that bond wasn't there.

So in 2018, I reached my "enough point". I realized that I wanted to feel more from the relationship with my mother. I called my mother and literally demanded that she listened to me without interrupting me. Through tears and a choppy voice, I told her how I was not happy with the current status of our relationship, that I did not feel like she knew me, I did not feel like she truly listened to me or saw me for me, that I didnt feel like I knew her, and that I truly did want a healthy mother/daughter bond....and she sat there and listened.

She stated that she shared the same sentiments in regards to wanting to have a healthy relationship and suggested that we just start from the beginning like strangers and converse with each other regularly. I told her that I am my own person and that if I made a decision in my life that she was confused by or didnt agree with that she should come to me and ask me, I would be glad to explain if I had the proper words. She agreed.

From that day, for about 5-6 months, we talked every day. Even if it was just a text to say good morning, we talked. I would call her for random things and I could tell that she liked that.

After a while, we shared more with each other and I began to understand how her thought process. I wouldnt get triggered when she would suggest, "Just pray about it" or said things that rubbed me the wrong way. I started to know her, what her love languages are, and I saw how much it helped. We are more open with each other now and things flow so much better.

Do we have the perfect relationship just over a year later? Absolutely not, BUT it is a DRASTIC difference to when we started. Any of my friends can attest to that. There are still times when she doesnt understand a boundary or when I do things, and there are time when I get frustrated with her, but at this point, I can see that she is actually trying. I also know that she is secretly ecstatic about our relationship because she is adamant on "not letting anything mess up the progress that we have made" (her words).

WHO IS THIS COURSE FOR?

This course is for
**the women with #MamaIssues who are tired of feeling the way they do &
are ready for positive change.**

This is for
the women ready to heal from a major thorn in their side.

This is for
**women who want to repair the relationship with their mother, but don't
know where to start.**

This is for
**women who are aware of and are taking steps towards breaking
generational patterns and "curses".**

This is for
women who are ready to do the work & dig deep.

This is for
women who are ready to drop the load & heal.

THE GOAL

I believe that a mother–daughter relationship is probably one of the most important bonds out there, it is one of the closest bonds out there. I feel that if more people heal this bond, the healing process for us, our mothers, and whomever comes after us the freer we become, the more we can show up confident in this world.

The ultimate goal of Healing the Bond | Mothers & Daughters is for you to be able to look at your relationship to your mother in a different and positive light. It is to use introspection, visualization, and the breath as keys to unlock your own answers. It is to gain more insight on yourself, your mother, and your stories. It is to build your psychological resilience. This course was created to give you tools in order to help you heal.

...& when you heal, your mother heals, your lineage heals.

MAIN DISCLAIMER

Please know that a present or alive mother is not NECESSARY for this work. I understand that many of you are not in (close) contact with your mothers, some of you have never met your mothers, or some of you have mothers who are no longer with us.

I also know that many of you have not had the best or healthiest of relationships with your mothers, hence you doing this work. I know that even thinking about your mother can cause your heart & breathing rates to spike.

If anything written here is too much, please take the time to breathe through it or PAUSE. Also feel free to use the sacred online community to vent/release. If you never knew your mother or you don't know the answer to these questions due to lack of information shared, you can answer intuitively or even base your answers on conversations that you have had with family.

If you get "stuck" on a question or if it is too overwhelming, it is okay to skip the question. I know that discomfort is a part of healing, but never do I ever want to cause PAIN.

Just like with yoga, we have to know when to be strong & when to soften, when to lean in & when to ease up.

KEEP IN MIND

1. The work lies within you; you are your own healer. I cannot heal you & this course cannot heal you, but I can help give you tools to dig, unpack, and actively work
towards healing yourself.

2. Results from this course will vary. What happened with my mother and I may or may not happen with the participants of this course.

3. If your mother is in your life, your healing is not based on whether or she wants to actively repair the
relationship with you. Know that this is YOUR work. You can only control yourself and how you respond to
situations in life. What is important to remember is that your goal should be for YOU to change, not for your mother to change.

4. Please do know and understand that this is just the beginning of the journey. Progress will take time. This process won't be perfect, but it will be worth it.

INTRODUCTION

In this course, we will be, essentially, doing root work. I will help you to dig deep within yourself. You will be unearthing a lot of suppressed feelings, emotions, and memories. The only way to heal is to go/grow through it. If you truly want to heal this part of yourself, this part of your life, you cannot go around it. There are no shortcuts. In all honesty, some questions, prompts, or visualisations may be too much for you at certain times. I want you to remember your breath in these moments and if it gets too overwhelming, pause for a bit, do what you have to do in order to find balance and come back to the work.

FLOW OF THE COURSE

· **Unearth + Uproot**: You start by asking yourself the tough questions and getting to where the good stuff is, underneath all of the pain, trauma, and attempts to cover it up.

· **Prepare the Seed**: This is the inner child work. Because of the nature of the issue at hand (a compromised, damaged, &/or broken mother/daughter relationship), you have to nurture the child within you. You will journey back to your child state in order to get answers and gain insight. You will nurture, love, communicate to, and listen to that child.

· **Hands in the Soil**: Hello shadow work! Dive into the depths and darkness of yourself and your family. You will address the parts that you often don't even want to talk about or the parts that you tend to hide, bury.

· **(re)Plant**: Re-examine how you view your mother and work towards truly seeing her. Use your own memories to bring that information forward. If you can see her, you can see yourself.

· **Nourish & Grow**: Open up your heart after all of the internal work. Discover and create pathways to acceptance. Now that you have a better view of your mother as a whole human, as a woman, you will figure out how you can start to make amends with the past and set yourself up to intentionally better your bond with your mother.

· **Harvest**: Now that you have done the internal work, you actually turn outwards and make efforts to reshape the relationship with our mother. You take steps towards reconnecting your bond. You grieve the mother you never had and the daughter you won't be. You create healthy boundaries. You integrate the healing in your life & the relationships outside of you. You reap the fruits of our labor.

WHAT YOU WILL NEED

Honesty

Courage

Compassion

Diligence

Patience

An open mind

A willingness to learn, change, &/or grow

A notebook exclusively for this work

part 1

UNEARTH + UPROOT

POSITIVE EFFECTS OF HEALING EMOTIONALLY

You cannot go back and change the past.
You cannot change your mother or what happened to her.
You cannot change what your mother did and did not do to/for you.
You cannot change the events that lead you to this point in your life.

What you can change and do have control over is yourself, your attitude, your insight, your perspective, and your ability to change and hold compassion for your mother. You have the capacity to actively work on your relationship and intentionally heal familial patterns.

TILLING THE SOIL

In the Unearth + Uproot you are going to dig up some feelings and thoughts that were buried. I will help you pull out the weeds, that have been acting like mental and emotional parasites, straight from the root.

Essentially, this is a preliminary section to figure out where you are, how much healing needs to happen, and where you want to be.

The questions asked may bring up feelings that you would rather not feel. The visualizations might make you really uncomfortable. Remember that I too have gone through this process, I am still going through this process and the only way to heal is to acknowledge what you feel!

Trust me, this little, temporary discomfort and irritation is better than a lifetime of pain and pent up trauma that can ruin other relationships and manifest as physical diseases.

When answering questions and doing exercises, write as much as you like or as little as you like. There are no wrong (or right) answers as long as you answer them honestly.

GET GROUNDED

Before we actually get started, let's take a few moments to ground.

Get fully aware of your surroundings and breathe.When you feel comfortable, close your eyes and take three deep, belly–filling, grounding breaths. Allow the air that you breathe in to flow through you and flow to all corners of your body. Allow it to fill you. On the out breath, allow all of your fears, worries, doubts and reservations to leave the body.

(If you need to take more breaths, light incense, or use essential oils to help you ground, please feel free to do whatever you need to do to help.)

Throughout this course, whenever you are feeling a bit anxious or your mind starts to wander, use these 3 breaths to bring you back.

ASK YOURSELF

Q1: What is the relationship with your mother currently like? Have you ever told your mother how you feel about your relationship, in a loving way? If so, how did she react? How did her reaction make you feel?

Q2: On a scale of 1-10 how close do you feel to your mother?

Q3: Why do you want a healthy relationship with your mother or at least a relationship that does not upset you?

VISUALIZATION: CHECK THE STATUS

Close your eyes. Take a minute to reflect on the relationship with your mother. Take a few deep breaths and imagine your mother standing in front of you.

Ask yourself: Am I inviting my mother closer to me or do I push her away? Do I feel as though my mother welcomes me or is loving towards me? How do I feel with her "standing" in front of me? How does my body feel? What are the thoughts that are going through your head? Is your mother's mere presence in your mind uncomfortable?

Take a few more deep breaths. In your mind's eye, imagine that your mother takes one step towards you. How does this make you feel?

As you continue to BREATHE, in your mind's eye, your mother takes a few more steps so that she is standing directly in front of you, less than an arms length away. How do you react? How is your breathing? What is happening in your body? What are your thoughts?

Take a few moments to feel how you feel. If you feel uncomfortable focus on your breath. Remember that you have the power, you have control, and it is all in your inhale and exhale. This is only an exercise.

When you are ready, flutter your eyes open, take a look around the room you are in and take three deep breaths to ground yourself.

Please write out what came up for you on the following page.

ASK YOURSELF

Q4: What would you change about your current feelings about/towards your mother? Please be as detailed as possible.

Q5: (for those who are still in contact with their mother) On a scale of 1-10 what amount of effort have you put into repairing the bond/relationship with your mother? Scale of 1-10 how much effort do you think your mother has put in?

Q6: What do you think are the right conditions in order to produce the most beneficial results (as far as improving your relationship)?

EXERCISE 1:
WHERE IS THE PAIN?

**"When we try to resist feeling something painful,
we often protract the very pain we're trying to avoid."**

-Mark Wolynn

In regards to the relationship to your mother, describe the pain that you are feeling, be it physical, metaphysical, emotional, mental, or spiritual. Describe the feelings and location. What pain are you avoiding or in denial of? Why?

ASK YOURSELF

Q7: How well do you think you know your mother?

Q8: (If you have ever known your mother or have family who would know your family history) What is the relationship like between your mother and her mother? Are there any patterns that you recognize?

EXERCISE 2:
DEAR MAMA

Write a letter to your mother starting with "Dear mom/mama/mother, I feel like _____". In this letter, express how you feel about her candidly and honestly. It is important to write in a non-accusatory way or a very harsh way. Even if you feel that your mother has wronged you, hurt you, or has "messed you up", speak more on YOUR feelings, your actions, your thoughts.

EX: "Dear mom, I feel as though we have not been close in a really long time and this really makes me upset. It hurts my feelings when you do not listen to me or when you yell at me. It makes me feel like an insignificant person. Although we don't really get along and we don't usually see eye to eye, I know that you've done your best to make sure that I survive in this world. I really hope that I can get to know you while you get to know me so that we can have a better relationship so that we can both heal and I won't pass down certain patterns to my children. Love, Jaz"

"Dear mother. Knowing that you gave me up for adoption makes me feel rejected and unworthy. I really wish I was able to get to know you and sometime's I wish we had a relationship. Most times, I have a really deep resentment & anger towards you, maybe even a hate. I hope that I can release that and some day forgive you."

Whether your mother is alive, transitioned, present, or absent, you can still write her a letter expressing exactly how you feel. You can read it aloud, save it, or even burn it.

UNEARTH + UPROOT | REFLECTION

How are you feeling? Are you feeling nervous or anxious? Are you excited?

What are your thoughts thus far? Is your Ego screaming, "WTF?" Are you hopeful?

Was there anything that came up that frustrated you or made you uncomfortable?

What is happening in your body? Do you feel any changes?

part 2

PREPARE THE SEED

A BOND THAT IS BROKEN

Most times the reason that we have the relationships that we do with our mothers is because there was a break in our bond, probably when we were really young and cannot consciously remember it. The bond/relationship was broken or interrupted and it was not fixed in an appropriate manner of time. When we are young, our minds and bodies do not recognize the trigger as something that was temporary or that the actions of our mother were not done in malice or ill will. When we are young we are dependent on our mother for our survival. Our bodies register this break/interruption as fear, abandonment, rejection, and essentially, it gets stored as "do not ever let this happen again or else you can die". Because a break occurred, we build defenses around ourselves in order to prevent whatever hurt us to ever happen again. We often put up barriers and even mental blocks to protect ourselves. Our mothers often do not recognize this and years, even decades go by, with a build up of triggers, defense mechanisms, and more trauma that further widens the gap between our mothers and ourselves.

INNER CHILD WORK

You are going to tap into your inner child mind and see if you can access some stored memories in order to help you understand where this all started. Once you get to the origin, you can better understand the complex relationship between you and your mother, have a better awareness of what is going on, as well as build up psychological resilience by realizing where some of your deepest and most ingrained triggers originated.

The child within you is still there and you just need to nurture her.
She will get the attention that she needs and deserves.

ASK YOURSELF

Q9: These are questions from Mark Wolynn's "It Didn't Start With You" to ask yourself when looking for an interrupted bond.

· Did something traumatic happen when your mother was pregnant with you?
· Was she highly anxious, depressed, or stressed?
· Were your parents having difficulties in their relationship during the pregnancy?
· Did you experience a difficult birth? Were you born premature?
· Did your mother experience postpartum depression?
· Were you separated from your mother shortly after birth?
· Were you adopted?
· Did you experience trauma or separation from your mother during the first three years of your life?
· Were you or your mother ever hospitalized and forced to be apart (incubator, tonsils removed, medical procedure? Did your mother need to have surgery or experienced complications from childbirth?)
· Did your mother experience a trauma or emotional turmoil during your first three years of life?
· Did your mother lose a child or pregnancy before you were born?
· Was your mother's attention pulled to a trauma involving one of your siblings (late term miscarriage, stillbirth, death, medical emergency)?

Another question that I might add is:
· Did your mother experience an interrupted bond (with grandmother)?

***Be gentle with yourself if you don't know the answer to any of these questions.
***Remember to breathe.

EXERCISE 3:
RECALL THE MEMORY

Recall the memory of when bond was FIRST broken. —the thing is that breaks in the mother daughter bond occur, often against our will, but we have to keep repairing it and mending it because if we dont our body/Ego will register it as a threat, as something we should avoid and never experience again, which pushes us away.

When recalling the first break in your bond, try to remember:
How old were you?
Where were you?
What happened?
How did you react?
How did you mother respond to your reaction?
What words would you use to describe this first break?

Bonus: If you are in a talking relationship with your mother, have her recall her memory of the first break in your bond. See if your accounts match up.

If you were adopted, or did not grow up with your mother in your life, you can recall how you felt when you found out that you were adopted or when you realized that your care-takers were not your biological mother (in the case of being in the care of grandparents or aunts/uncles).

VISUALIZATION: WITNESS THE BREAK

Find a comfortable position to sit or lay in (***do not lay in the bed). Make sure that wherever you are is a place that you consider safe. Take a few deep breaths. Allow your body to relax. Loosen your jaws. Relax your tongue from the roof of your mouth.

If you need to, allow your exhale to draw out a little longer than your inhale. Give yourself permission to go into the depths of your subconscious mind. Take a deep breath and let it out.

Close your eyes and imagine that you are standing next to yourself as a child. You witness a break in your bond with your mother. It does not have to be the first one, but one that you remember vividly and feel strongly in your body.

(We are going to talk in present tense to call the energy of this energy to the now, to make it clear.)

What is happening? Where are you? Are there any scents that stand out? Do you hear anything? Is any physical harm being inflicted on your body? What is your brain telling you? What are your thoughts? How do you feel? What is happening in your surroundings? What do you do/how is your body responding (are you crying, are you frozen, are you feeling confused, are you breathing)? How does the mechanisms your brain devised to protect you in that moment show up in your life today?

EXERCISE 4:
NURTURE THE CHILD

Let's work with your inner child. What comforting words would you say to your three year old self in this process, with these feelings (without dissociating, avoiding, or ignoring what is coming up)? What would you have said to your three year old self as she was experiencing the breaks in the bond with your mother?

Here are some examples:
"I got you baby girl."
"It's not your fault."
"I am here for you."
"I won't let you go. You're safe in my arms."
"Your feelings are valid."
"I know you're scared, but I promise to not let go."
"I won't leave until you say its okay for me to go."

EXERCISE 5:
STIR UP THE GOOD

Our bodies and our minds more easily store "negative" or painful experiences than positive, happy ones because our Ego wants to protect us. Ego wants to remember the harmful things in order to prevent those things from happening again. Although traumatic memories are easier to recall than pleasurable ones, the body and the mind still hold them as well. It might take a bit more patience and work to bring the happy thoughts back up.

Recall good/positive/warm feelings or memories of or with your mother. Bring the positive experiences from your childhood to the forefront. What were the smells/scents & sounds? What was around you? What colors can you see? Who was there with you? How did your body feel, what were the sensations? What were you thinking in your mind at that time? Can you remember what was sad? It could be a snapshot or it can be a full recap of an event. Write out as many as you can remember.

How does remembering this/these moments make you feel?
How does it feel in your body right now?

ASK YOURSELF

Q10: How can you nurture your inner child from this day forward? How will you treat her? What will you say to her? How can you acknowledge her? How can you love her?

HAVE FUN

The inner child loves without fear. Having fun comes naturally to her, she doesn't even have to think about it!

There is no shame and guilt here. You are free and we are safe to express ourself through movement, however we see fit!

The goal of this exercise is to activate the root and sacral chakra. You want to loosen up the areas of stagnation or blockages. You want to shake the limbs, releasing pent up energy. You want to build up a sweat. YOU ARE GOING TO DANCE IT OUT, laughing and smiling. Sing like no one is listening. Play whatever lights up your body that makes you want to move. Use headphones or speakers. Do what you want!

Write how you feel afterwards.

EXTRA CREDIT HOMEWORK

If the relationship with your mother allows for it, ask her about the relationship between you two during the years that you cannot remember.

My mother told me that I weaned myself from her breast at 3 months old and she felt so rejected by me. That single event shaped our relationship and how she viewed me. She took it as I didnt want her, love her, or need her. As an adult, certain words and reactions would come up. I didn't know where they came from. My mother also experienced abandonment (from a baby-8 years old). She never developed a proper relationship with her mother in her formative years because my grandmother left her in Jamaica with my great grandmother, while she (granny) went to America.

PREPARE THE SEED: REFLECTION

How are you feeling at this part of the process?

Have your feelings changed? Do you feel more or less optimistic?

How do you feel about the relationship towards yourself, towards inner child now?

What came up for you that was interesting? Was there anything that was brought to the surface that frustrated you or made you uncomfortable?

What is happening in your body? Do you feel any changes?

part 3

HANDS IN THE SOIL

SHADOW WORK

People often think of shadow work as a thing to be afraid of. In reality, shadow work is just addressing and healing from the things that we would much rather keep in the dark, away from the forefront of our attention. By ignoring the shadows, more damage than good is done. The Shadow is still a part of you. Avoiding the shadow is avoiding a part of yourself that hold so many answers, so many keys to open the doors of your healing.

Essentially, this whole program entails shadow work, but I will help you dig into & expose things you might not want to talk about and the things that might sound cringey if said aloud.

ALL feelings and emotions are welcome in this section and for the whole course. They are all useful and serve a purpose. Please do not suppress whatever comes up for you. Note them and do your best to process, release, or transmute them. It is not "bad" to feel lower vibrational emotions and sensations, afterall, we are having a WHOLE human experience.

Please remember that there is no guilt or shame here. Honesty is how you are going to get yourself to the land of health.

Again, if you have never met your mother or you do not know her side of the family's history, use your intuition & inner-knowing.

ASK YOURSELF

Temperaments, attitudes, and behaviors do not always come from our own life experiences. Our ancestors play a part in not only our physical traits, but our emotional, psychological, and even spiritual traits. It's way more than skin deep.

Q11: What behavioral, temperamental, or situational patterns come from mother or your mother's side of the family? (Quick temper, need to be in control, having a child with a man that is emotionally unavailable)

Q12: What are some things you wish your mother had done for you or had done differently?

Q13: Have you blamed your mother for not loving you how you thought you should have been loved? Why do you feel this way? What are you comparing her love for you to?

EXERCISE 6:
DESCRIBE YOUR MOTHER

(Adapted from Mark Wolynn)
In this exercise, describe your mother how you remembered her growing up & how you remember her now. Describe her temperament and how you felt about her. Also, write out EVERYTHING you blame your mother for. Don't hold back. Don't be afraid. Be honest.

Start each sentence with:
"My mother was...."
"My mother is...."
"I blame my mother for...."
"My mother irritates me when/because...."

ASK YOURSELF

Rejection, which is a product of anger, is often the easier or more available option for humans. It takes more energy to hold compassion than it does to "hate" someone or something in someone.

"Anger is often an easier emotion to feel than sadness...
It was easier to reject her [mother] than to love her."
– Mark Wolynn

Q14: What do you reject about your mother? Why? What about her bothers you? Why?

Q15: Who in your life reflects what you reject in your mother? How can you learn how to heal from this relationship in order to help the relationship with your mother?

Q16: What do you reject in your mother that resurfaces in you (temperaments, habits, decisions made)? How does this make you feel?

VISUALIZATION:
INNER CHILD LET DOWN

For those of you who have experienced your biological mothers, go back to a moment where you feel your mother let you down or you felt betrayed by her.

For example, in 5th grade, I told my mother that I liked a boy in my class. I was really excited about it. She told me that I didnt really like him, that it was "puppy love". I was confused because I knew I liked him, but she told me I didnt. She completely burst my bubble. Before I told her, joy was running through my body, after I told her, I felt deflated and sad. In that moment where she invalidated my feelings towards the opposite sex, I felt like I could not trust her with sharing my feelings, especially my "intimate feelings". I stopped telling my mother about who I liked and who was my boyfriend. I felt as though if I told her, she would steal my joy.

What were the sensations in your body? What did you do? What was she going through? What was happening at that time, in your lives? What conclusions did you come to & how did that play a part in shaping your relationship today?

Please write down what came up for you.

SPEAK YOUR TRAUMAS

"Once we have the story, were more able to revisit an experience–even a trauma– without reliving all of the turmoil attached to it"

"Without language, our experiences often go "undeclared" and are more likely to be stored as fragments of memory, bodily sensations, images, and emotions."
– Mark Wolynn

When you do not express or discharge our traumas, they get trapped and stored in the body. When we were younger, we didn't have language to formulate our traumas into words so they, instead, got shelved away in our minds and engrained in our bodies. That's why when something triggers us, it is so painful. We keep reliving the experiences instead of releasing them.

Sometimes, I feel like being triggered is so overwhelming because the trauma WANTS to be released. It wants to escape the body and the body wants to purge it. Instead we get physically addicted to these feelings because of the chemicals released in our bodies (as read in Breaking the Habit of Being Yourself by Dr. Joe Dispenza).

EXERCISE:
SPEAK YOUR TRAUMAS

Speak the personal trauma(s) that you have experienced with your mother and declare the story/your story so that you do not have to continuously relive the trauma in your body.

If you want, you can write them out and then actually verbalize what you wrote out. Another thing you can do to aid in releasing is to shake it out. While standing up, you can bounce around (feet need not leave the ground if this causes too much strain to slightly jump), shake one leg at a time, and shake out your arms and legs. You can even do this to music that makes you happy!

If all of this feels good to you, you can write out other traumas that have nothing to do with your mother and repeat the process!

ASK YOURSELF

Q17: What are your trigger symptoms? (These are alerts/signals that we still have room to heal)

Q18: What happens in your body when you feel like your mother, has triggered you, when you have conversations about your mother, or when people talk about their relationship with their mother around you?

Q19: When you reject your mother (or something that she does or did) what do you do (yelling, distancing, etc)? How does your body react?

Q20: What is your instinctive mode of operation in your mothers presence or when you think/talk about her? Are you naturally defensive, do you feel like you have to protect yourself, are you removed, dissociative, aloof, angry, dismissive, shrinking?

EXERCISE 7:
WHEN YOU, I FELT

Let's practice making the traumas "tangible".

By writing these statements out, it provides another way to put feelings into words. Think of examples when you felt like your mother did something to you, that triggered you, that hurt you, that made you feel low. Write out how her actions made you feel.

"When you _____, I felt _____."
or
"When you _____, I feel _____."

Ex: "When you don't listen to me, I feel like me and my opinions do not matter" or "When you forced me to take that class, I felt like I didn't have a choice and from that moment it made me feel like other people had the right to make decisions in my life and have control over me."

HANDS IN THE SOIL REFLECTION

How did you feel about shadow work and what we did in this part of the course? Is shadow work a little less intimidating?

Did you have any moments or questions that were a bit difficult or uncomfortable for you to address? What were you able to do that helped you ground and continue?

At this point, how do you feel about the process?

What sensations are happening in your body?

part 4

(RE)PLANT

INTRODUCTION

Let's explore what you know about your mother. I will help you work on seeing her in a different light, seeing her as a human that was, and still is, having human experiences.

Our mothers are a part of us; we cannot deny that or try to ignore that fact AND attempt to heal, simultaneously. Healing comes from acceptance of what was, what is, & the integration of what is inevitably us. What will not help the healing process is avoidance, ignorance, and separation.

ASK YOURSELF

Q21: Do you know if your mother struggled emotionally, physically or psychologically in your youth? If you were aware of her state, did it hurt you to see her suffering? Did you want to take her pain away? Did you try to take her pain away, how?

Q22: In your life today, do you struggle similarly to how your mother struggled? Do you recognize your mother's pain in yourself? Is there a pattern between you two?

Q23: Do you know your mother's trauma? Her mother's trauma? Do you know of the trauma that occurred between your mother and her mother?

EXERCISE 8:
RELEASE THE JUDGEMENT

By releasing the inner judgement that stems from your mother, it frees you from the self-judgement. What you judge your mother for often shows up in you. For example, my perception my mother was that she was strict, controlling, harsh. That consequently has shown up internally and & I am the same way with/towards myself. I felt like my mother always has something negative to say about everything & I internalized that. I tend to do the same thing to and with myself (be strict harsh & or controlling).

What are some traits that you judge your mother for? Do the things that you hate in your mother also show up in you (unintentionally)? If so, how can you release the harsh and unforgiving judgement that you have cast on your mother? How can you love yourself enough to release this passive self–harm?

Even if nothing transfers from your mother to you, what are some judgements you've held against your mother that you can release?

VISUALIZATION: SEE HER STORY

Just like in "Sensing the Vibe", imagine your mother standing in front of you, a few steps away. What sensations do you feel in your body that you are aware of?

Now envision your mother taking a few steps away from you and turns to face you. As you look at her, she begins to be surrounded by all of the traumatic events that she has ever experienced. Even if you don't know exactly what harm has transpired in her life, try to imagine what she could have gone through based on how she interacted with you, the things that you have heard or stories that she has told you. Imagine what she had to do to protect herself and to stay alive.

Take three deep breaths.

Now see your mother as a young woman, a small child, or even a small baby experiencing all of those traumas, that pain, that hurt.

How does this make you feel in your body? What sensations and and feelings come up for you? Where do they manifest in your body? Can you sympathize or empathize with her, what she went through, or what she felt? Does this make you emotional? Are you able to hold compassion for her? What would you want to tell the younger version of your mother? What would you tell your mother now?

ASK YOURSELF

Q24: Have you ever thought that your mother could not give you what she never had, what she never received, what she was not aware of? That she was doing the best that she could?

Q25: What can you forgive your mother for right now?

EXERCISE 9:
REWRITE THE STORY

You are going to (re)write the story with your mother. You are going to form healing sentences for your mother. Express how you feel, honestly. Incorporate any new revelations, moments of appreciation, sympathetic sentiments, and your desires. While being transparent, please do consider your mother's feelings. Take into consideration the exercises that we have done thus far and what they have brought up for and in you.

Ex: Sometimes it is difficult to express my emotions to you, but I would like to work on changing that. You have always done your best, and even though I have not always realized that, thank you. I get nervous around you and I would like to feel comfortable around you. I would really love for us to be able to spend quality time together and enjoy each other's presence without getting mad at each other.

Please write in a way that you would be able to share this with your mother at some day, if/when you are ready, if your mother is still alive.

EXERCISE 10:
CREATE THE THINGS

Create sentences (mantras), rituals, practices, exercises around new narratives, in regards to your mother, that you wish to embody and manifest. You can start with 1-3.

For the mantras that you create, do something physical as you say them help further engrain them in your mind. Ex: rub heart center, rub earlobe, rub space between thumb and index finger.

Examples of creating the things would be:

HEALING SENTENCE
"The relationship with my mother is healthy and I feel safe around her."

EXERCISE
Whenever I talk on the phone with my mother,
I light incense so the scent keeps me grounded.

RITUAL
Before I step foot in my mother's house,
I take three deep breaths and rub my necklace.

What you create does not have to exactly mimic what is written above, but these are these are the general concepts.

VISUALIZATION: CHECK THE STATUS

Close your eyes. Take a minute to reflect on the relationship with your mother and if you feel differently towards her at this point in the course. Take a few deep breaths and imagine your mother standing in front of you. Ask yourself: Am I inviting my mother closer or do I push her away? Do I feel as though my mother welcomes me or is loving towards me? How do I feel with her "standing" in front of me? How does my body feel (tight, relaxed, holding breath, nervous/anxious)? What are the thoughts that are going through your head? Is your mother's mere presence in your mind uncomfortable?

Take a few more deep breaths. In your mind's eye, imagine that your mother takes one step towards you. How does this make you feel?

Also you continue to BREATHE, in your mind's eye, your mother takes a few more steps so that she is standing directly in front of you, less than an arms length away. How do you react? How is your breathing? What is happening in your body? What are your thoughts? Do you feel differently from the first time we did this exercise?

Take a few moments to feel how you feel. If you feel uncomfortable focus on your breath. Remember that you have the power, you have control, and it is all in your inhale and exhale. This is only an exercise.

When you are ready, flutter your eyes open, take a look around the room you are in and take three deep breaths to ground yourself.

Please write what came up for you.

BONUS HOMEWORK

This is not mandatory, but it can add to the knowledge you have in regards to your mother's experience.

If you are in contact with your mother, ask her questions about her life (including traumas [physical, emotional, mental trauma, deaths in family, trauma in the workforce, trauma in every day life, miscarriages, abortions, etc.]) and be open to answers. Be gentle. Work your way up to harder and more possibly triggering questions. Maybe, you might have to ask questions over a period of time. Ask in love, receive in love. Truly listen. Really see her. Even if she doesnt answer right away or fully, let her sit with it. It may be something she buried in shame or grief for YEARS. She may not have the language or courage to share immediately. She may be caught off guard or shocked or surprised. Remember, you are not obligated to know anyones story. That is a privilege. She may respect you for wanting to even hear her or listen to her story or want to get to know her in a different way, on a different (intimate) level.

REPLANT
REFLECTION

How are you feeling at this point in the course?

What are some of the thoughts going through your head?

.

.

Has your views towards your mother changed since the beginning of this course? If so, how?

Did you learn anything about your mother?

What is going on in your body?

Was there any revelatory moments that happened for you?

part 5

NOURISH & GROW

INTRODUCTION

In this section, I will help you use what is, right here and right now, in front of you. Clues from the past will still be used, but your focus is on your current mind state. Look at yourself and your mother as you are, as she is, where you both are. You are honest with yourself and practice acceptance as well as non–attachment.

ASK YOURSELF

Q26: If you are in contact with your mother, is she still in pain today? What is hurting her?

Q27: In what ways can you see/acknowledge your mothers humanness? In what situations did your emotions/ego prevent you from seeing your mothers humannes? How does this make you feel now?

In most cases, mothers just want to be a mother to her children. They want to be there for them and nurture them, but somewhere down the line, there was a disconnect and a rift that never got repaired. **of course this is not the case for every mother**

In the cases of adoption or abandonment, even though your mother was able to conceive you, she wasn't able to properly provide for you. In her mind, for whatever reason she thought that her choice was justified and valid (for whatever reason). As crappy as her decision was, she is still your mother.

What does this bring up for you?

ASK YOURSELF

Q28: How can you be at peace with what you received (physical things, attention, love) and what you did not receive from your mother? How can you forgive your mother for intentional and unintentional pain they may have caused in your life?

Q29: Have you forgiven you mother for how she was unable to love you in the way that you wanted her to love you?

EXERCISE 11:
CLEAR THE NARRATIVES

Ego is a very useful part of human nature, especially in situations that threaten our lives. In many adult lives, Ego gets way more control over our lives than it is supposed to. The Ego tends to conjure up scenarios that probably won't ever happen, but because it has been fed for so long, because it has gotten so strong, the fear of these imaginative scenes holds us captive and prevents us from any forward/upward movement.

Write down all of the worst case scenarios that your brain is coming up with or as come up with since the start of this course. Write the fears. ALL OF THEM.

Tell Ego "Thank you for protecting me, but these fabricated situations are illusions, they are not real nor do they have to be real. Ego, I recognize that you are a vital part of my being, but I release you from being in control of situations that do not pertain keeping me alive. I release you from putting fear in the way of my freedom. I thank you for keeping me alive thus far and getting me to this point. I will call on you when I actually need you."

EXERCISE 12:
ASK FOR WHAT YOU WANT

Write down a list of everything you want out of your relationship. This, in a sense is a list of polite demands. (For those with mamas that you are in communication with, you can hold on to this list until you feel that your mother is truly ready and able to hear you and to comply.)

What you write will be the outline for the boundaries that you will set for yourself in relation to your mother.

Examples:

"I would like for us to be able to not argue with each other every time we are in the same room."

"I would like for you to actually listen to me."

"If you don't understand something I do or say, please do not chastise me or make fun or me. Please ask me for clarification."

If your mother is no longer with us on this earth or if you have no contact with your mother, you can still do this exercise!

ASK YOURSELF

If these questions are not applicable, please feel free to bypass this page.

Q30: What is something you can do right now to better your relationship with your mother?

Q31: What do you admire about your mother?

Q32: In what ways can you extend compassion to your mother?

LOVE LANGUAGES

Love Language #1: Words of Affirmation

Love Language #2: Acts of Service

Love Language #3: Receiving Gifts

Love Language #4: Quality Time

Love Language #5: Physical Touch

EXERCISE 13: LEARNING THE LANGUAGE

Do you know what your mother's love languages are?

My mothers is acts of service and words of affirmation. (She wants/likes to be told good job)

If it is not obvious to you what your mama's love languages are, listen to what she is saying when she speaks to you and pay attention to the underlying message. Listen to what your mother asks you for.

When my mother asks me to do her hair, it isn't that she wants me to do her hair, she more than likely sees it as a bonding moment and a way for us to be physically close.

If you have a communicative relationship with your mother, you can also ask her what her love languages are.

Mothers are humans too, and often times, they might not know how to or feel comfortable asking for what they actually want OR they might be nervous and fearful of rejection if they are direct.

Once you have identified your mother's love languages, **what are your love languages?**

If your mother has transitioned, see if you can use your memories to recall what your mother's love languages could have been OR ask family members/friends for help.

If you have never met your mother, you can imagine what her love languages were/are or if you know people who knew your mother, you can ask them for insight!

BONUS HOMEWORK

If you are in communication with your mother, ask her if she would like to actively participate in rebuilding your relationship and if she does, let her know that it will take equal work from both parties to create a successful and healthy relationship. Remember the internal healing only comes from you. As you heal, you will naturally change, but for your mother to change and heal, be gentle with her as well as yourself.

"CAN YOU ACCEPT THE NOTION THAT ONCE YOU CHANGE YOUR INTERNAL STATE, YOU DON'T NEED THE EXTERNAL WORLD TO PROVIDE YOU WITH A REASON TO FEEL JOY, GRATITUDE, APPRECIATION, OR ANY OTHER ELEVATED EMOTION?"

– DR. JOE DISPENZA

NOURISH & GROW REFLECTION

How are you feeling now?

What is your level of optimism?

What is your view on your mother now?

Did you have any difficulties seeing her humanness?

Were there any blocks that you had to work through?

part 6

HARVEST

INTRODUCTION

You have done most of the work, and focused internally.
Now you get to the work outside of yourself.

This is the final stage, the final stretch. If you are not yet ready to reap the harvest, that is okay. There is no need to rush.

Harvest is where you actively practice unconditionally loving your mother and by doing so you unconditionally love yourself.

Remember that this is a PRACTICE. You are going to mess up, falter, backslide, etc., but again, it is your job to be diligent in this work. You can have your partner, friend, sibling, or even your mother hold you accountable for getting back in the ring and giving it all you got. All that I ask of you is to be consistent, and even when you "mess up" be loving and gentle towards yourself. Also, please ask you mother to be loving and gentle with you during the process, and take one step at a time.

Ps. It's okay to feel nervous or anxious. You are doing something different. You are journeying in uncharted territory. Remember to breathe and know that freedom is on the other side of fear.

ASK YOURSELF

Q33: How can you stay soft (physically) when thinking of or being around your mother?

Be aware of your body language, sensations, and feelings in the body when you talk about your mother or when you are with her. (Maybe you can repeat that visualization of her as a child with all of her trauma and see if that helps).

LOVE LANGUAGES

Q34: Do you think that you can fully attune back to your mother? If so, how? If not, why?

Q35: What has your mother (whether alive or not) revealed to you throughout this process? What have you learned about yourself?

BOUNDARIES ARE YOUR FRIENDS

Please remember that this relationship is now between two adults. You have a different mindset and you have to gently explain to your mother that although you will forever be her daughter, you are not a child. This is another part of the process that is necessary. HELP your mother understand that you are not a child.

Do not be afraid to put up boundaries. Setting boundaries is in no way pushing your mother back out. This is preserving the state of your mental, emotional, physical, and spiritual well being.

Be vocal about your boundaries in a respectful way. Once you set your boundaries, you have to verbalize them and let them be known! What good is a boundary if no one knows about it? Once you share your boundaries, you can then hold whomever you told accountable for crossing that boundary.

Remember that silent boundaries are **USELESS!**

EXERCISE 14:
BUILD THE BOUNDARIES

Even if your mother is not physically in your life, you can visualize her presence OR if you are open to ancestral veneration, you can communicate to the spirit of your mother.

Let's get to setting these boundaries. Imagine how you want to feel within these boundaries. Write out a few words to reflect how your boundaries make you feel (Ex: strong, safe, protected, etc.)

Start out every boundary with:
In/with this boundary I _____

"Create space for me to breathe"
"Honor my space"
"Give myself permission to be at ease"

Once you finish writing your list, say your boundaries aloud.
How does it make you feel?

BUILD LIKE YOU MEAN IT

Build up the relationship with your mother like you would with a romantic or plutonic relationship — like you are two people who don't know each other, but want to get close to each other. Essentially, you two ARE strangers and you need time to get to know each other as two adults who have lived their own separate lives.
I know that we are more than likely not our mother's friends and we would not consider them our friends. If we had the choice, we probably wouldnt be friends with our mothers, let alone have them in our lives…but we chose to come in to this world through them, so we have to figure out the lesson in them & learn it.

Be vulnerable and share certain things from your past. Who knows, there might be similar stories or patterns that can help you both see the humanness.

For those of you who have mothers who have transitioned, you can still set boundaries with her. If you ever feel like your mother's spirit is feeling overbearing, loud, or is just making you uncomfortable, you can lovingly say to her something along the lines of:

"Mom, I know you love me and you want to be near me, but right now this is too much. I will designate a time & space when you can come to me. I am doing the work to heal myself and I need to have healthy boundaries between us. I have not forgotten you."

 If you have never been able to meet your mother, you can visualize what a healthy relationship with boundaries would look and feel like.

SEPARATION IS NECESSARY

For those of you who have a decent or working relationship with your mother.

Sometimes we are so "close" to the relationship with our mothers or so close in proximity that we cannot fully see each other (which in turn we cannot agree or come to terms with each other). We end up suffocating each other, not giving each individual the space to be, breathe, process, collect themselves, and be respectful to one another. Even plants need proper space from each other so that one does not smother the other.

What is your healthy distance in relation to your mother? (Seeing her once a week, once a month. Calling her every other day, texting her daily) How can you put healthy distance between your mother and you to broaden your perspective of your perception of each other? Determine the degree of separation that is needed for this relationship to grow.

I know that my mother and I do WAY better when we do not live together and when we have breaks in the times that we spend with each other. Maybe the distance does make the heart grow fonder or maybe the physical space allows us to not have to be so defensive with each other (I am an Aries and she is a Capricorn...those horns often ram against each other). Maybe your relationship needs to be repaired while in close proximity with each other. Figure out the appropriate space that is needed, or needs to be taken, (boundaries) in order to have the most positive effect.

EXERCISE 15:
PULL FROM THE PAST

If you have ever had a healthy or happy relationship with your mother (whether she is still alive or not), please do the following exercise.

If you have never met your mother or if you cannot recall any happy/pleasant moments, you can either skip this exercise or use your inner–child imagination to conjure up a scenario that you would have loved to share with your mother.

Think back to something you know you enjoyed doing with your mother. Ask her if she would like to do that again. As a grown woman, I asked my mother to cuddle with me and hold me and her eyes lit up. Maybe for you it was walking you around the park, making cookies together, or dancing, but pull from a time when your relationship was good, & doing it today, can help start the process of regrowing your relationship.

Ask your mother for something (the thing that we thought of in plant/replant) that may seem childish/child-like, but brings you joy and brings you back to a feeling of connectedness & love with your mother, maybe even before the bond was broken/relationship was damaged.

Even if you don't LOVE doing whatever it was from your past at this moment, maybe rekindling that memory will spark something in you or your mother that can show your body that good things do happen with your mother.

VISUALIZATION: SEE THE FUTURE

How do you see your relationship with your mother in one year, two years, five years, ten years? What can you do and continue to do in order to actualize what you see in your minds eye? (Remember that if you can see it and feel it, it is already yours, you just have to vibrate at the same frequency in order to bring your vision to your present reality)

Imagine what the relationship between you and your mother looks like in 5 years, in 10 years. How has it changed? How has it improved? How does this relationship affect the other relationships in your life?

If your mother is in the spirit realm, in what ways can you bond with her as an ancestor? How can you allow her to show up as a mothering spirit? Can you trust her knowledge now that she as access to the spirit world? How can you honor her essence (can you incorporate her photo or item she loved in an altar)? **Remember that as an ancestor, our family members hold great worldly & spiritual knowledge. They do not carry the same energy they carried on earth.

If you have never met your mother, do you want to meet her?
Do you want to reach out to her? Do you want to have a relationship with her? Are you at peace with her physical presence not being in your life? How can you be a better mother or mother figure to your yourself and the people around you?

VISUALIZATION: CHECK THE VIBE

If your mother is present in your life and you both have agreed to reconcile your relationship, before arranging to meet up or talk with her, please do this visualization as many times as you need to.

Visualize your mother standing in front of you one last time.

Take three deep breaths and imagine your mother standing in front of you. Be aware of any changes or sensations in your body. How do you feel towards your mother? How does your mother feel to you, is she warm and inviting or cold and pushing you away?

Take deep breaths and imagine your mother taking a step towards you. How does this make you feel?

Now, in your mind's eye, your mother takes a few more steps towards you and she is now standing only a few inches in front of you.

How does this closeness make you feel? What are the sensations in your body? Does this still feel uncomfortable for you? Do you want to reach out and touch your mother?

If this last energy check feels way better and more comfortable than the first time we did this visualization, know that you have released or transmuted some major trauma(s) from the body and you are well on your way to being healed from the break(s) in the bond with your mother, on your way to freedom.

If it does not feel any better, if the same sensations and thoughts keep coming up in your head, just know that you need a bit more patience and time to work through what is still stored in your body. Do not fret. Everyone's healing journey is different. Some people have a more accelerated journey while others have a slower journey. Neither speed is right or wrong, it just is. Keep loving yourself in the process. You will get there eventually. I have faith in you.

EXERCISE 16:
DEAR MOM, I FEEL

Write out a "Dear mom, I feel as though____" letter encompassing everything you have learned thus far. Be as honest as you can and also be as gentle as you can.

You can write a "Dear mom, I feel as though" letter to a mother that is deceased or that is absent. You can choose to read it out loud, burn it & release it, or keep it. The choice is yours!

How has this "dear mom, I feel" changed since the beginning of the course?

COMMUNICATION IS LITERALLY KEY

Communication is going to play a huge role in the process of repairing the relationship between you and your mother.

A question that you have to ask yourself is,
"WHAT IS MY COMMUNICATION STYLE?"

How do you feel most comfortable communicating and how do you like being communicated to?

Next, you have to figure out your mother's communication style. Maybe you know already, you might have a good idea, but it is best to actually ask her how she likes to be communicated to.

For example, I like to write (or text) first to get all of my thoughts and points out and then have an actual conversation. My mother prefers talking it out straight.

Please be mindful and aware of non-verbal communication. You or your mother can be triggered by certain gestures, noises made, or even eye contact (or lack thereof).

Also, please know that if the relationship is not stable just yet, it is okay to have a mediator or neutral person there, but make sure that both parties consent and know who will be present.

BONUS HOMEWORK

Have a sit down with mother and both of you take turn sharing something with each other that you haven't shared before, or share in detail about something you superficially told her about. This can also be done over the phone if being with your mother in person is not an option for either of you.

You also have the option to share your answers to prompts and whatever you wrote in your journal/notebook with your mother.

ASK YOURSELF

Q36: How has your opinion or viewpoint of your mother changed since the start of this course?

Q37: What is the relationship with your mother like now?

Q38: On a scale of 1-10 how close do you feel to your mother?

BONUS EXERCISE: HEART TO HEART

This is an exercise that may take some time and courage to work up to. This involves actual close contact with your mother.

What you want to do is stand directly in front of your mother. (If standing is not available, sitting is fine, just make sure that you are eye level; no one is higher than the other)

Take a few deep breaths into the belly, your mother can do the same. As you breathe, actually look into each other's eyes for a few moments. You can do this for a few breaths or for a few minutes. It might feel a bit uncomfortable, you might feel a bit exposed or vulnerable, but stick with it. Remember, your mother might be feeling the same exact way!

After looking into each other's eyes, embrace each other,
HEART TO HEART

Hold each other in silence. Listen to each other breathe. Feel each others heart beats. Give yourself and your mother permission to be and feel safe in this embrace. Allow your body to soften on every out breath. If tears begin to flow, please allow them to fall.

This is a very powerful and intimate exercise. If you are not ready for this level of intensity and closeness, that is perfectly fine. There is NO rush or pressure to YOUR process & timeline.

IT MAY NOT END WELL

Let's be real. Some mothers will not be here for this process. So what to do if your mother is unwilling or unable to take accountability, actively participate, want to change, or is not in the picture because we have completely removed them from our lives to preserve our mental health?

• Continue to breathe through whatever feelings may come up.

• Do not take YOUR MOTHER'S actions personally. Know that her decisions are not your fault and they have nothing to do with you.

• Remember that fear (of the unknown) is one hell of a drug. Admitting certain things to you, let alone to herself, can open a whole can of worms that she is not prepared for.

• Accept wherever your mother is at this point in her life. Continue to love her as best as you can despite her sh*t. Extend compassion and love. (please know that this can be done at a distance).

• Continue to do your own work to unpack whatever patterns still may be buried deep. Continue self-reflecting & introspecting.

• Keep nurturing your inner child.

• Know that you have tried and you have put in the energy to do right by this relationship. That is more than enough.

• Focus on yourself and what you CAN do.

• Continue sharing your story (& remember that your story is not to be confused with Who You Are).

• Lean into the nurturing relationships that ARE present in your life.

• Seek out a therapist if you need one. There is NO shame in going to therapy!

• By showing up for yourself & continuously loving & healing yourself, you heal her too, whether she admits that to you or not.

• KEEP HEALING & remember that you are only responsible for yourself.

• Celebrate YOUR wins, victories, and progression. Be your biggest cheerleader.

HARVEST + COURSE REFLECTION

YOU DID IT!
YOU MADE IT!
YES, SIS!

How does it feel to have completed the course?

.

How do you feel about your mother and your relationship with her?

.

What were some amazing moments?

Were there any overwhelming moments?

Did you have any major realizations or revelations during the course?

What are your overall thoughts?

END NOTES

You deserve to be happy.

You deserve to live fuller lives and have more than your mothers, grandmothers, etc.

You deserve to expand into your fullness and your fullest expression of love.

Just because this course is over, DOES NOT mean that the work is over. Maneuvering & growing from this relationship is going to be something that you will have to continually work on. You will be tried and tested, but that is okay, remember that everything is a lesson. If you need community support, please either reach out to your sisters in the forum or be on the lookout for in-person and virtual meetups via my newsletter and social media posts. Know that you are NEVER alone! Keep breathing through it.

I will be opening up one-on-one coaching sessions for Trauma with Your Mama. If you want a personal accountability partner and for me to work closer with you, please use this dicount code "**HELPME50**" on my website to receive $50 off of the service.

THANK YOU

Thank you for trusting me.
Thank you for sticking through this.
Thank you for showing up for yourself, your health, your emotions, your journey. I am really proud of you. I know there were moments of WTF & I can't do this, but here you are at the end of this course wiser, braver, and more psychologically resilient than ever!

I hope that this course has truly helped you and has proved to be an assistance in your life. My prayer whenever I share an offering is that whomever partakes leaves better and more sure of themselves than when they started.

XO,
J. Chavae

Made in the USA
Columbia, SC
09 August 2019